WINGS APART

BURT
KIMMELMAN

WINGS APART

BURT
KIMMELMAN

DOS MADRES
2019

DOS MADRES PRESS INC.
P.O.Box 294, Loveland, Ohio 45140
www.dosmadres.com   editor@dosmadres.com

Dos Madres is dedicated to the belief that the small press is essential to the vitality of contemporary literature as a carrier of the new voice, as well as the older, sometimes forgotten voices of the past. And in an ever more virtual world, to the creation of fine books pleasing to the eye and hand.

Dos Madres is named in honor of Vera Murphy and Libbie Hughes, the "Dos Madres" whose contributions have made this press possible.

Dos Madres Press, Inc. is an Ohio Not For Profit Corporation and a 501 (c) (3) qualified public charity. Contributions are tax deductible.

Executive Editor: Robert J. Murphy

Illustration & Book Design: Elizabeth H. Murphy
www.illusionstudios.net

Typeset in Adobe Garamond Pro
ISBN 978-1-948017-33-6
Library of Congress Control Number: 2018967596

First Edition
Copyright 2019 Burt Kimmelman
All rights reserved. No part of this book may be reproduced or transmitted in any form or by any means graphic, electronic or mechanical, including photocopying, recording, taping or by any information storage or retrieval system, without the permission in writing from the publisher.
Published by Dos Madres Press, Inc.

ACKNOWLEDGEMENTS

Special thanks to Thomas Fink, Barbara Henning, Sherry Kearns, and Stephen Paul Miller for reading and commenting on these poems at various times. The editors of the following publications have my gratitude for issuing some of the poems in this book, often in earlier versions of them: *Golden Handcuffs Review; Hambone; Like Light: 25 Years of Poetry & Prose by Bright Hill Poets & Writers*; and *Marsh Hawk Review*.

And very special thanks to Robert and Elizabeth Murphy for their continued support of my work, for their brilliant renderings of it in several Dos Madres Press volumes.

Author photo by Jane Kimmelman, copyright 2019.

For Diane and Jane
Tot iorn meillur et esmeri

TABLE OF CONTENTS

To Live —— 1
Threesome —— 2
Caught Bird —— 3
Day's End, Summer —— 4
Autumn, Maplewood —— 5
The Death of Jim Tolan —— 6
Puget Sound Ferry to Victoria, June —— 8
Birthday Poem —— 9
Sky —— 10
Life on a Sunny May Morning —— 11
Yom Kippur 5777 —— 12
Dawn —— 13
Summer, Morning —— 14
Slavonice Café on a May Evening —— 15
It Happened —— 16
Marcel Broadthaers at the MoMA —— 17
Marriage —— 18
Hlavny Nadrazi, Praha —— 19
May Day, Marina —— 20
Asleep on a Train —— 21
Bar Mitzvah Photo, Terezin Ghetto —— 22
Summer Afternoon —— 23
The Freedom We Feel —— 24
Asana —— 25
A Summer Rain at *The Mount* —— 26
A Round Robin —— 27
Summer Solstice, Early Evening —— 28
Film Noir —— 29

About the Author —— 33

WINGS APART

TO LIVE

Branches reach up
in their silence,
on the tips their
violet blooms.

Midsummer heat
and bright sun, when
our flowers are
all forgotten.

Yet at dusk I
find them in their
cool beauty, rare,
brief radiance.

Their burgeoning,
one of summer's
kindnesses, is
all I can know.

THREESOME

The day you
were born I
heard your cry.

CAUGHT BIRD

One of our cats
walks the backyard
fence, in his mouth
a bird he sets

beneath a bush.
Our other cat
joins him to watch —
caught by branches,

the bird thrashing,
then scurrying
free. As one they
leap to chase it,

running it down.
The spent bird killed,
I watch the leaves
flutter in sun.

DAY'S END, SUMMER

Lace blossom
the bee rests
upside down.

AUTUMN, MAPLEWOOD

for Samuel Menashe

How lonely the life
asleep, the breathing
quiet, even — an
open window — I
listen in the dark.

THE DEATH OF JIM TOLAN

> "… with an entrechat
> perfectly achieved"
> — William Carlos Williams, from "The Artist"

The news arrived, as expected after
holding on for three years. The funeral
was held in crowded Brooklyn — a rainy
cold Saturday. Over drinks, bites of food,
we talked while photos of a life spooled through
a TV screen. We sat down to watch, the
closed coffin nearby. There had
been "massive organ failure." Friends and
family were arranging themselves to
begin the formal remembrance. The night before

I was sitting at a Manhattan bar,
waiting for the jazz cabaret downstairs
to open. The cavernous room was mobbed
with people freed from work on a Friday —
but I had my stool and my glass of beer
was just right. Two kids next to me tried out
the barbecue, sipping fancy drinks. The
bartender was keeping his pace, always
moving. He knew about crowds. I saw it
all work through him. He was an artist. I

was lucky to be there. He was pouring
some red liquid over ice, then something
clear though syrupy. With one hand he squeezed

half an orange into a strainer, shook
it, added in the juice. He twisted a
slim peel of lime into a tight spiral
he set floating on the surface. There were
instruments — a long silver stirrer, a
small grater he would use to scrape dust from
a nutmeg held at the ends of his pursed

fingers. He moved gracefully along the
bar — a dancer looking young. He could shake
a drink with his one hand while teasing the
customers, pouring with his other. He
filled beautifully stemmed glasses with brightness
to the brim, not a drop left over. He
set drinks at the end of the bar for the
waiters, dispensing his largesse. Squaring
his shoulders, he eased back up my way. He
knew what he was doing. This was the night.

PUGET SOUND FERRY TO VICTORIA, JUNE

We rock and sway in waves
a ship makes crossing our
bow — a stolid island

in the strait, its sand cliffs,
pine trees — some gulls flying
beside us, in a row.

BIRTHDAY POEM

> "I walk in the slow rain,
> never less accomplished, never happier."
> — Harvey Shapiro

I read Grace Paley's stories as I sit
below our backyard maple tree and think
of how I never scare people like she
could with resentment and tenderness, deep
down, her love more than people could expect.

I take solace in the tree's shade on this
unusually hot morning, squirrels
and birds high above me, our cats prowling,
my seventieth birthday, happiness
in the offing, a fortuitous moment.

SKY

Wings apart
the bird floats
above trees.

LIFE ON A SUNNY MAY MORNING

Light through the trees,
birds are singing–
squirrels aloof,
cats are prowling.

From a distance,
among the leaves–
a stabbing plaint,
again, again.

YOM KIPPUR 5777

Mother, father,
brother now gone,
I speak for them,
not knowing death.

DAWN

The night is when
our dreams mingle
thought and desire,
until dawn when

the light takes us
back from the earth
where we return
in our longing.

SUMMER, MORNING

> ". . . li auzel
> chanton chascus en lor lati."*
> — Guillem IX of Poitiers

I awake
to the heat
of the day —

cicadas
winding their
long moment —

children, birds
singing in
their pleasures.

*"[. . .] birds / sing out the first stave of new song [. . .]"
("Ab la dolchor del temps novel"). Trans. Paul Blackburn

SLAVONICE CAFÉ ON A MAY EVENING

The cold is strange comfort
all of a sudden — when
it sets in on the square.

The buildings come alive,
their etched tableaux — glowing
stone in the setting sun.

IT HAPPENED

It happened in
the usual
way and somehow
never again.

MARCEL BROADTHAERS AT THE MoMA
NEW YORK CITY, FEBRUARY 2016

"*Mur*" "*bois*" "*PORTE A*"
"*anti-chambre*" "large?"
"*isolée*." Air,
water dissolve

our scratchings.
We walk on land,
but where do we
belong — surely

not in words, books
we imagine.
The sea's heart beats
and so the wind

takes flight. We read
the mollusk's shell —
and the egg's, its
fragility.

MARRIAGE

Making love
sorrows and
joys are one.

HLAVNY NADRAZI, PRAHA*

The ticket agent — her bright red
hair, red dress, rose tattoo inside
her arm — tells us where we must go,
the track where we wait for our train.

We glide into the sun — look back
at the castle's spires, beveled
red roofs, bridges, river winding
through it all — the city awake.

*Main Station, Prague

MAY DAY, MARINA

Trees along the river's
inlet, their leaves, no wind,
the spring cool today, I

never know why I sit
looking at them like this,
my rustle in stillness.

ASLEEP ON A TRAIN

On the long ride
she soon tires
of the passing
trees, hills and lakes.

Her shoulder leans
into the seat,
her eyes closing,
the journey's end.

BAR MITZVAH PHOTO, TEREZIN GHETTO

The clothes of the Jew,
yarmulke, tallis,

a boy looks into

the camera, his
picture left behind.

SUMMER AFTERNOON
PONTIGNANO, TUSCANY

Beneath the shade
beside the road

cicadas whirl,
spires of pine.

THE FREEDOM WE FEEL

"Rather, night...."
— William Bronk

Lamplights show the way
up the boulevard
until the city
becomes a bright blur.

At night stars lead us
nowhere unless there
is some place to go
though not knowing how.

The "stars in time" are
there for us to read
one or another
tale we never knew.

What truths they tell us
are their real stories
and we follow them
to find our way there.

The endless world is
another matter
yet that is where I
would give up my life.

ASANA

I press my body
back on its haunches
and bow to the ground
to breathe in and out,

knowing forgotten.

A SUMMER RAIN AT *THE MOUNT* LENOX, MASSACHUSETTS 2018

for Ed Foster

The shadows in the pines
are darkest in the rain,

soft green limbs bowing down,

no wonder what woods hold,

all we want beneath
the hidden sun, slate sky.

A ROUND ROBIN

In July the red streaked
sky lies over dark hills.

December's sunset turns
our bare maple tree gray.

April's birds sing early,
sun rising, fill the world.

October's birds begin
their silence, leaves falling.

. . . .

July's birds sing sunset
to its soft conclusion.

SUMMER SOLSTICE, EARLY EVENING

I sit watching
the light on leaves,
their shine — the sun
still high above.

I hear a bird
close by somewhere,
its song — and then
many at once.

FILM NOIR

> for Charles Borkhuis, "darkness is never enough"

I love old movies, their turmoil in black and white
on a dark evening, a rainy street, a single car
the size of a trolley parked out front of a townhouse —
the only way to know someone is living somewhere.

In that building a guy has murdered a man who was
choking him, who found he was having a drink with his
girlfriend in her apartment who, panicked, handed him
the scissors she left lying beside her sewing box.

She's beautiful, like in the portrait of her displayed
in a gilt frame that sits in the window of a store
just across the alley from a swank restaurant where
the guy, that night, dined with some people he knew in town.

Afterward, on the way to his hotel he sees her
there in the painting, but then he hears her ask him if
he likes it — the her in the painting now the woman
waiting in the alley's shadows for him to pass by.

The dead man was never much of a lover, she says,
standing over the corpse — stabbed in the back just because
someone fell hard for a painting — and we know why he'd
kept her all alone in her art-deco apartment.

The guy's a professor at a leafy college north
of the city, a married man who lives with idylls
in quietude — who has suddenly realized he must
fight for his life and get rid of a dead man's body.

He wraps it in her blanket, carries it down her wet
brownstone steps in the opaque rain, stuffs it in his car
and drives off, but the cops pull him over since the guy's
forgotten, in his haste, to turn on the car's headlights.

In the heavy rain the one cop asks for his license,
and there's a letter from the Board of Education
in the guy's wallet, which the cop reads, water dripping
from his cap, telling him "Next time, Prof, turn on those lights!"

The guy's feeling pretty good, but he'll leave tire tracks
and foot prints near some woods, where a boy scout trips over
the body the next day — and it turns out the dead man
was a town father, but the killers know his secret.

Unplanned, even perfect, crimes always go wrong because
crimes always do, because people just don't realize they're
living in a wrong world, because they kid themselves, but
I know the facts — and I don't want to see the ending.

Tired anyway, I turn off the movie — but, let's
face it, the world's not simply black and white, and I don't
mean to say the world isn't gray, because I know it
is, though it's also as red as blood, as green as her eyes.

Why can't life be like Keats's "Ode to Autumn" — no doubt
a poem the professor taught, until his whole world
no longer made sense — a poem about desire,
really, what we're all born into, innocent at first.

Homicide is simple, people simple — poetry
not so simple, as it bestows a story we need
in which no one's in trouble — like in a movie when
the world's good and it makes sense, but then it all goes wrong.

ABOUT THE AUTHOR

Author Photo by Jane Kimmelman

BURT KIMMELMAN was born and raised in New York City after the Second World War. *Wings Apart* is his tenth collection of poetry, following *Abandoned Angel* in 2016, and *Gradually the World: New and Selected Poems* in 2013. His poetry is often anthologized, and has been featured on National Public Radio; a number of interviews of him are available in print or online. Kimmelman has also authored books and articles mostly on literature, some on art and architecture, and some memoir. He is a professor of English, teaching literary and cultural studies at New Jersey Institute of Technology in Newark, New Jersey.

Other books by Burt Kimmelman
published by Dos Madres Press

There Are Words (2007)
The Way We Live (2011)

He is also included in:
Realms of the Mothers:
The First Decade of Dos Madres Press - 2016

For the full Dos Madres Press catalog:
www.dosmadres.com